This book belongs to:

The Gardening club

Please Keep in the Greenhouse

Young Discoverers

PLANT LIFE

SALLY MORGAN

Kingfisher

KINGFISHER
An imprint of Larousse plc
Elsley House, 24-30 Great Titchfield Street,
London W1P 7AD

First published in 1996 by Kingfisher

10 9 8 7 6 5 4 3 2 1

A CIP catalogue record for this book is available from the British Library.

ISBN 0 7534 00480

Editor: Molly Perham
Designer: John Jamieson
Art editor: Val Wright
Author: Sally Morgan
Consultant: Michael Chinery
Photo research: Elaine Willis
Cover design: John Jamieson
Illustrations: Peter Bull p. 17 (bot.), 18 (left), 19 (right), 20, 25 (left), 27; Richard Draper p. 16, 21 (left), 24; Angelica Elsebach p. 22-23, 26 (left), 26 (top), 26-27; Nick Hall p. 4-5, 5 (centre top). 8; Ruth Lindsay p. 6 (left), 6-7, 30 (top), 30-1; Chris Orr p. 4 (left), 5 (right), 8 (top left, bot. right), 9 (top left), 10-11, 11 (top left); Eric Robson p. 14-15, 15 (right), 28 (top), 28-29, 29 (top); Michelle Ross p. 10 (left), 18-19, 24 (bot.); Richard Ward p. 7 (right), 9 (bot.), 11 (right), 12-13, 15 (top), 21 (right), 23 (right), 29 (bot.), 31 (top right).
Photographs: Bruce Coleman p. 9 (Hans Reinhard), 10 (Carol Hughes), 13 (Eric Crichton), 14 (Jack Dermid), 21 (Eckart Pott), 23 (Alain Compost), 27 (Hans Peter Merten), 28 (Hans Reinhard); Ecoscene p. 4, 7, 19, 20, 31; Nature Photographers Ltd p. 25 (Paul Sterry); NHPA p. 17 (George Gainsburgh).

Printed and bound in Spain

About This Book

This book looks at how different kinds of plants grow and reproduce themselves, and explains how essential they are to the survival of all living things. It also suggests lots of experiments and things to look out for.

You should be able to find everything you need for the experiments in your home, at a local garden centre, or in a garden, park or nearby woodland. Do not collect flowers or plants from the wild, even if there are lots of them.

Activity Hints

- Before you begin an experiment, read through the instructions carefully and collect all the things you need.
- When you have finished, clear everything away and wash your hands.
- In a special notebook, keep a record of what you do in each experiment and the things you find out.

Contents

All Kinds of Plants

There are over 380,000 different kinds of plants, and they are found in all but the very coldest parts of the earth. There are plants in the oceans, too. We recognize most plants easily, because they are green. The colour comes from green pigment called chlorophyll. Plants range in size from tiny single-celled algae to giant redwoods and Australian eucalyptus trees that reach more than 100 metres. Some plants live for just a few weeks, others live for thousands of years.

Tallest Plants

The giant redwoods of North America are some of the tallest plants in the world, reaching heights of more than 100 m.

Seaweeds

Seaweeds are marine plants. They do not have proper roots and stems. Instead they have a holdfast, a root-like structure that attaches them to rocks, and fronds that bend with the currents.

Plants can be divided into groups. Algae, which include seaweeds, are the simplest plants. Mosses and ferns are primitive land plants. Conifers are a group of large, cone-bearing plants. The most advanced plants are the flowering plants. Their flowers produce seeds and fruit. They include the broad-leaved trees.

Eye-Spy

Many different types of plants can be found in parks and gardens. Try to find an example of a plant from each group.

Parts of a Plant

Each flowering plant has a shoot with stems and leaves, and a root system under the ground. Flowers are produced at certain times of the year and these turn into fruits and seeds.

Making Their Own Food

Plants are different from other living organisms because they make their own food by photosynthesis. This process takes place in the leaves, where there is lots of chlorophyll. Some photosynthesis also takes place in green stems. Plants have many leaves, to trap as much light as possible. During the day the chlorophyll absorbs light energy from the sun. This is used to turn carbon dioxide and water into sugar, which is used to fuel the plant's growth. Sometimes the sugar is stored as starch. The gas oxygen is released into the air. Oxygen is needed by animals and plants.

Eye-Spy

Not all leaves look the same. There are simple, compound, and prickly leaves. Compound leaves have several leaflets. Look for different leaf shapes and draw them in a notebook.

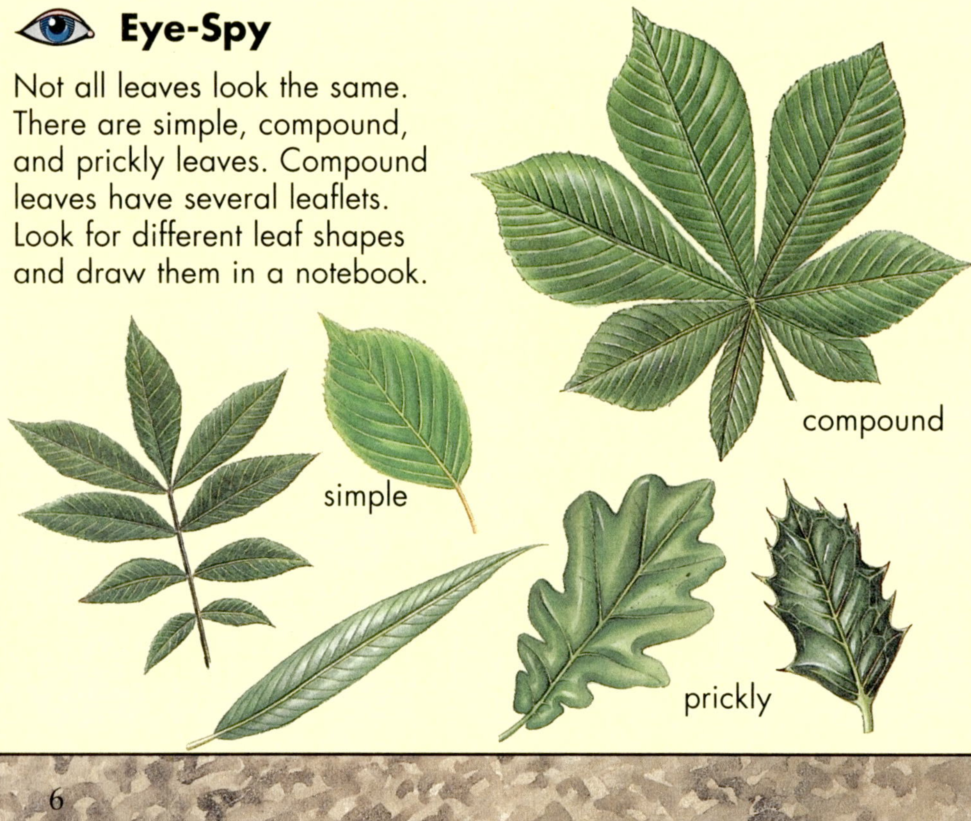

Largest Leaves

The huge floating leaves of the giant waterlily are the world's largest simple leaves, often reaching 2 m across. They are supported by ribs that radiate from the centre, like spokes on a wheel. The leaves are so strong that they can support the weight of a young child.

Do it yourself

See how a runner bean seeks the light.

1. Put a runner bean seed in a pot of compost. Water the compost and wait for the seed to grow.

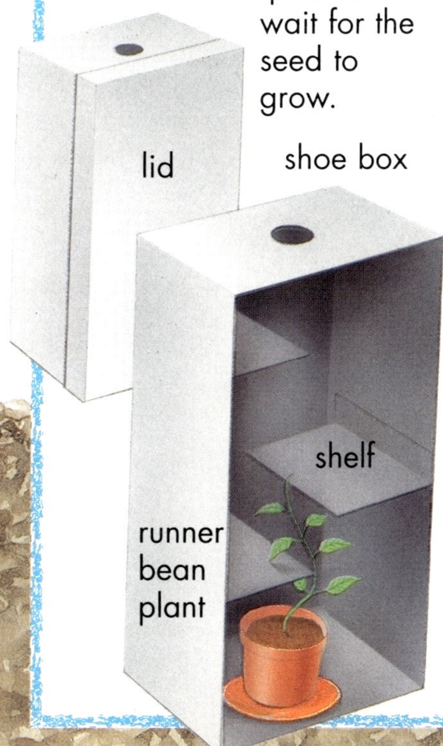

2. Take a shoe box with a lid and cut a hole in one end. Paint the inside of the box and lid with black paint.

3. Using smaller pieces of card, position the 'shelves' as shown in the diagram.

4. Stand the box so that the hole is at the top. Put the young runner bean plant inside and replace the lid.

5. Every few days, open the box and water the plant.

How It Works

The runner bean detects the dim light coming through the hole and grows towards it. Plants make sure that their leaves are in the best position for photosynthesis.

Meat-Eating Plants

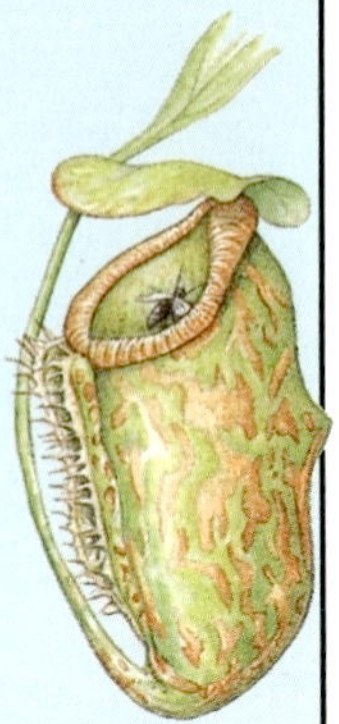

When a fly falls into the liquid inside a pitcher plant, its body is dissolved and this releases nutrients for the plant.

When an insect lands on the sticky leaf of the Venus fly trap, it struggles to get free. The leaf then snaps shut and traps the insect inside.

Light is essential for plants – without it they would become yellow and have stunted growth. They also need nutrients from the soil, especially nitrogen, phosphorus and potassium. Farmers make sure that plants get sufficient nutrients by adding fertilizers to the soil. Fertilizers contain balanced amounts of nutrients, to get the best possible growth from the crops.

One way to make sure that plants get enough nutrients is to add decaying plant matter or manure to the soil. This is mixed into the soil so that the roots can absorb the nutrients.

Eye-Spy

Not all leaves are green. Make a note of the different coloured leaves of pot plants in your home. Some plants from tropical countries have red pigments as protection against the strong sun.

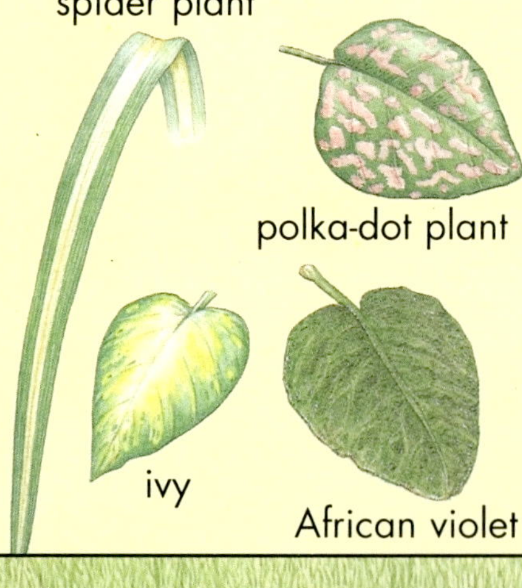

Leaf Mosaics

The leaves of a tree are carefully arranged in a mosaic pattern, so that they do not shade each other.

Changing Colour

In the autumn the leaves of deciduous trees change colour from green to shades of yellow and red as the chlorophyll breaks down. Finally, the leaves fall. New green leaves form from buds in the spring.

Do it yourself

Discover how important nutrients are to the growth of plants.

1. Fill a small margarine tub with sand. Fill another tub with sand mixed with a teaspoonful of slow-release fertilizer. Firm the sand in each tub with your hand. Water both tubs.

2. Sprinkle grass seed evenly and cover with a thin layer of sand. Place the tubs on a sunny window ledge and water them regularly if they dry out.

3. Measure the height of the grass each week and compare the colour of the leaves.

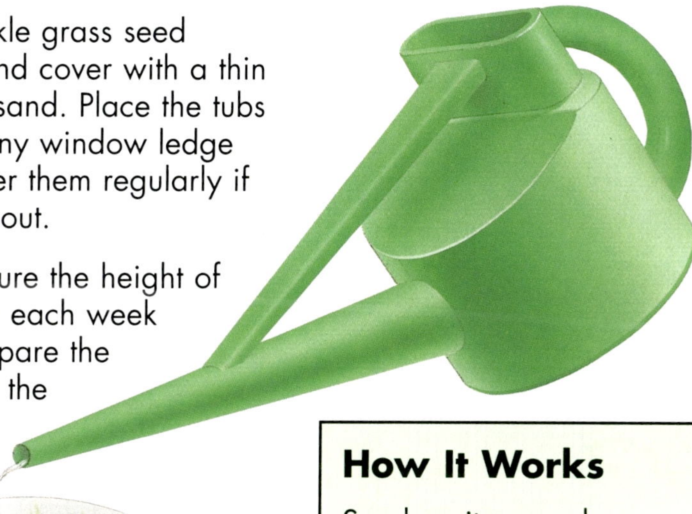

tub with sand

tub with fertilizer and sand

How It Works

Sand on its own does not contain nutrients, so the grass growing in just sand will not grow well. The leaves will be yellow and short. Fertilizer provides the grass with nutrients, so it will grow taller and the leaves will be a healthy green.

Roots

Roots hold a plant firmly in the ground and absorb water and nutrients from the soil. Some plants, like dandelions, have a sturdy tap root that extends deep into the ground. Others, like grasses, have a network of fibrous roots that spread out around the plant. Just behind the tip of each root are a mass of tiny root hairs. These increase the surface area of the roots to absorb as much water as possible. Some roots are used to store foods, such as starch. When this happens, the roots swell up and become tubers.

Deepest Roots

Roots can extend deep into the ground to find water. The deepest roots ever measured reached a depth of 120 m. They belonged to a wild fig tree like this one growing in South Africa.

Eye-Spy

When you next visit the supermarket, see how many vegetables there are that come from the root of a plant.

dandelion (tap root)

Underground Storage

Roots and bulbs often become swollen as sugar is moved to the roots and stored as starch. The plant uses the food store in spring, to send up new leaves and flowers.

Do it yourself

Grow a new geranium plant from an old one.

1. Break off a side shoot where it joins the main stem.

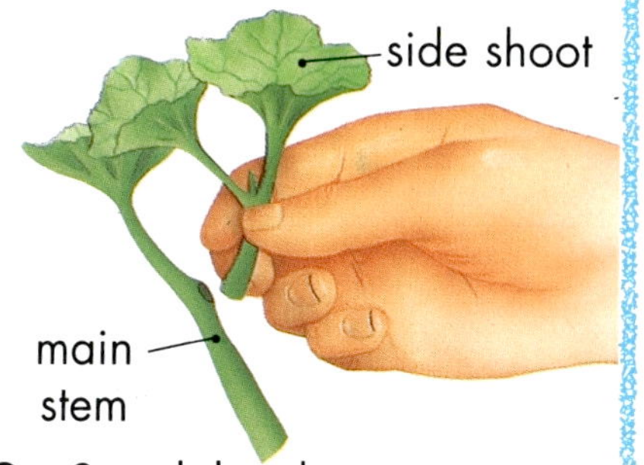

2. Stand the shoot in water and leave it on a window ledge until roots have grown.

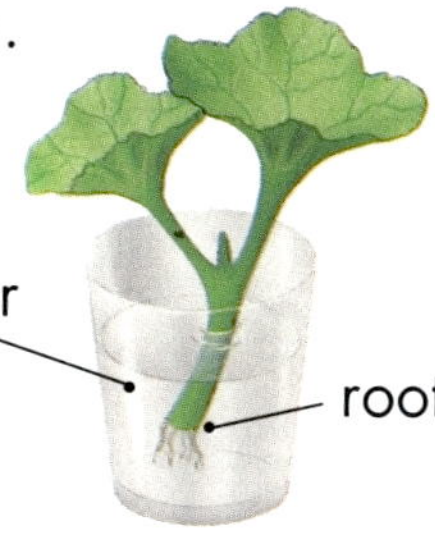

3. Plant the rooted shoot in a small pot of compost. Place a plastic bag around the pot to keep the air moist.

Inside a Plant

Plants have to be able to move water and food from the roots to the leaves, and from the leaves to the growing tips. Inside a plant there is a system of tubes. Water is absorbed by the roots and is moved through the tubes up the stem to the leaves. When the water reaches the leaves, some is used in photosynthesis, but most evaporates from the surface of the leaves. This process is called transpiration. Sugar is carried in phloem tubes from the leaves to wherever it is needed for growth. Sugar can be moved both up and down the plant, whereas water moves only one way.

Transpiration

If a plant loses too much water, it wilts. A beech leaf loses far more water than a laurel leaf which has a waxy, waterproof upper surface.

Do it yourself

Colour a flower by putting it in water tinted by ink.

1. Carefully split the stem of a white flower such as a carnation.

2. Support the flower so that one part of the stem is in blue-coloured water and the other is in red water.

3. Gradually the veins in the white petals will become coloured.

During the day, water evaporates from the surfaces of leaves. Trees have thousands of leaves, and the largest trees can lose as much as 1,000 litres of water each day.

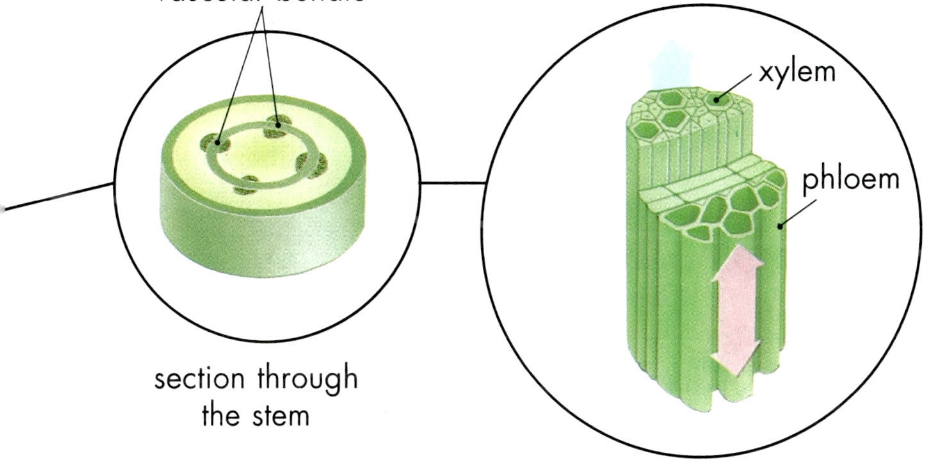

section through the stem

vascular bundle

A complex network of tubes connects all the parts of the plant. In the stem, the phloem and xylem are found close together in a vascular bundle. The vascular bundles form the veins, which can be clearly seen in leaves. When water reaches the leaves, some may enter the choloroplast to be used in photosynthesis, but most of the water evaporates from the surface of the leaves. Water from the xylem vessels moves through the air spaces in the leaves and out through holes called stomata.

Do it yourself

Leaf rubbings make interesting pictures.

1. Lay a leaf face down on a table. Put a piece of white paper on top.

2. Using the side of a crayon, rub over the leaf so that the pattern of veins is visible on the paper.

Plants in the Food Chain

Plants are essential to the survival of all living things. They are producers, because they are responsible for making food. Animals are consumers, because they eat plants. Some animals, called herbivores, eat only plants. Other animals, called carnivores, eat the herbivores. In this way, plants and animals form food chains. If anything happened to the plants, there would not be enough food for the herbivores and they would starve. So would the carnivores.

Plants have ways of protecting themselves from herbivores. Just a touch of this poison ivy may cause a nasty skin rash. Some trees have thorns, and nettles are protected by stinging leaves.

Do it yourself

Dead leaves and plant matter can be broken down into compost.

1. Make some wire netting into a circle and support it with canes.

2. Line the bin with sheets of newspaper. Place your kitchen and garden waste in the compost bin.

3. Cover the top with a piece of old carpet and leave for a few months.

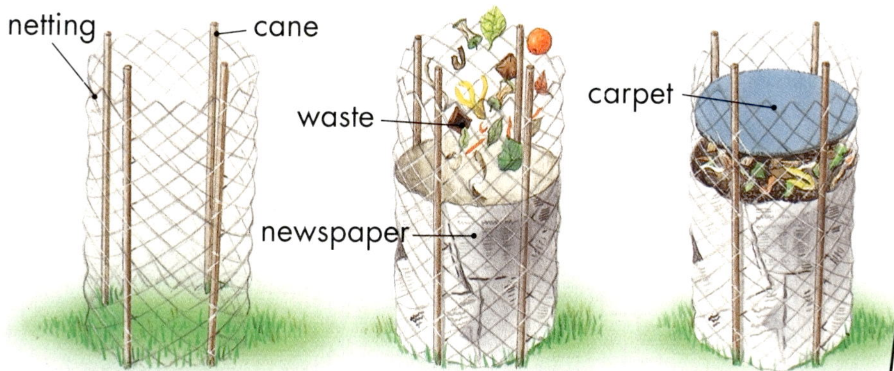

How It Works

As micro-organisms start to break down the plant material, they release a lot of heat. The carpet and newspaper help to trap the heat, speeding up the breaking down process. After a few months, you should have a rich organic compost that can be put back into the soil.

Death and Decay

Plants need nutrients for healthy growth. Fortunately, these nutrients are recycled, so they never run out. The remains of plants and animals are broken down by bacteria and fungi and the nutrients are returned to the soil.

Plants as Food

Plants are an important source of food, and they make up a large part of our diet. The three most important plants are rice, maize and wheat. These plants are large grasses and they are called cereals. Cereals are useful plants, because they produce seeds that contain the starch and protein that we need. Wheat seeds are ground up to make flour, while rice and maize can be cooked as they are. In many parts of the world, people survive on a totally vegetarian diet that contains only plants, with no animal food at all.

Most of the world's richest soils are used for growing cereal crops. Cereals are often grown in huge fields with no hedgerows. The crops are collected by enormous combine harvesters.

Medicinal Plants

For thousands of years plants have been used to reduce pain, heal wounds and cure illness. The bark of the cinchona tree produces quinine, which is used to treat malaria. Digitalis made from foxgloves may be used to treat heart disease. Rheumatism may be treated with drugs made from the autumn crocus, and leukaemia with drugs from the periwinkle.

periwinkle

foxglove

autumn crocus

cinchona

Scientists look for better ways of growing crops. These tomatoes receive a mixture of nutrients to ensure maximum growth.

Do it yourself

Potatoes are good to eat because they are full of starch, which provides energy.

1. In spring, dig over a patch of ground and plant a potato tuber that has begun to sprout.

2. When the shoot is about 15 cm tall, pile up earth around the stem. Continue to do this as the plant grows.

3. Late in summer, the plant will begin to die back and you can dig up the new potatoes. Use a fork, but be careful not to spike any potatoes.

Trees

Forests are very important to the atmosphere, because trees use up carbon dioxide and produce oxygen. Unfortunately, many forests have been felled for their wood, and many types of trees are in danger of dying out. Wood is a versatile material that is used for fuel, timber and furniture. Two of the most prized woods for furniture-making, teak and mahogany, come from the rainforests.

Eye-Spy

Many household items are made of wood. How many examples can you find? Look at the colour and the grain of the wood. Can you guess what type of tree it came from?

Oldest Trees

Some of the oldest trees in the world are the ancient bristlecone pines which are found in the United States. They may be as much as 5,000 years old.

What Type of Tree?

Conifers produce cones and have needle-like leaves that stay on the trees all year round. Deciduous trees usually have broad leaves and drop them in the autumn.

Trees form a green canopy high above the rainforest floor, shading the plants and the ground below. Climbing plants form a tangled mass of 'ropes' around the trees, and orchids and bromeliads grow on the branches.

Do it yourself

You can learn a lot about a tree by taking a few measurements.

1. Wrap a tape measure round the trunk of the tree about 1.5 m above the ground.

Annual Rings

When you look at a tree stump, you can see growth rings. There is one for each year of the tree's life. By counting the rings, you can work out the age of the tree. In a good year, a tree will lay down a wider ring than in a poor year. By studying the rings, biologists can work out what the weather was like in the past.

2. Make a note of the measurement in centimetres. This is the circumference. Divide the circumference by 2.5. This gives you the age of the tree in years.

3. Look for girdle scars on a twig of the tree. The distance between two girdle scars is the amount of growth produced by the tree in any one year.

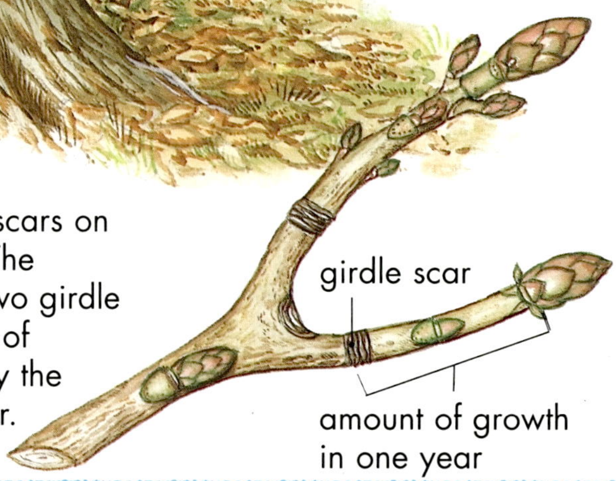

Plants in the Desert

Deserts are dry places that receive very little rain. Daytime temperatures can soar to 30°C, but at night the lack of clouds means that the temperature may fall to 0°C. Few plants can survive such harsh conditions – those that do are specially adapted. Cacti have thick, fleshy stems and spines instead of leaves. Other plants appear if there is rain and live for just a few weeks.

After rain, seeds in the desert soil germinate and a carpet of flowers appears. The flowers quickly produce seeds.

Do it yourself

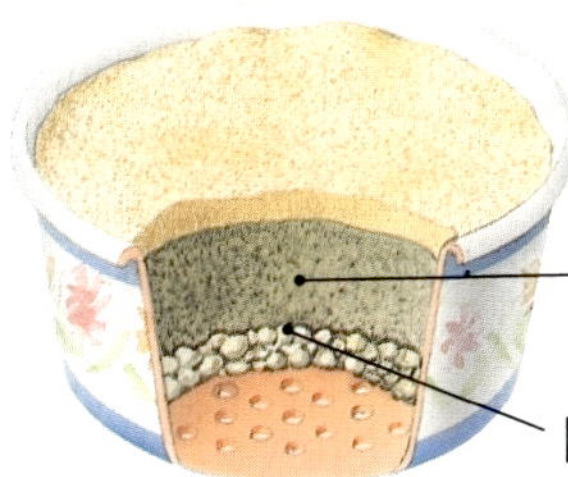

Cacti are easy to grow and you can keep several types in a small bowl.

1. Put a layer of pebbles or gravel at the bottom of a bowl, then fill it with sandy compost.

2. Plant your cacti and finish off with a layer of gravel. Give your cacti a little water and place the bowl near a sunny window.

Flowers

Flowers contain a plant's male and female reproductive organs. Most plants have both male and female organs in the same flower, but a few have separate male and female flowers. Male organs, or stamens, make a powdery yellow dust called pollen. Female organs include the stigma and ovary. To make a seed, pollen has to travel to the female stigma in another flower. This process is called pollination.

Where Do Our Garden Flowers Come From?

Many garden flowers have been bred from wild flowers. The wild pansy has a small flower, but the garden pansy produces large, brightly-coloured flowers.

Largest Flower

The rafflesia plant has the largest and smelliest flower of all! For pollination it attracts flies by creating the smell of rotting flesh.

Do it yourself

Pressed flowers are great for greetings cards.

1. Lay a sheet of blotting paper on a piece of wood or thick cardboard. Position the flowers on the paper so that they do not touch. Put a second piece of blotting paper on top, and then another piece of wood and some heavy books.

2. Leave the flowers for several weeks until they are completely dry. Carefully lift the flowers from the blotting paper.

Look-Alikes

The flower of a bee orchid looks just like a bee. This disguise is so life-like that real bees are encouraged to visit the flower and in doing so pick up the pollen.

Plants need help in transporting pollen from the male stamens to the female stigma. Bright colours are an advertisement, telling birds and insects that there is sugary nectar inside the flower. As they collect nectar, they brush against the stamens and are covered in pollen. When they visit another flower, the pollen is rubbed off onto the stigma, completing pollination. Once the pollen is on the stigma, it grows a tube down to the ovary and fertilizes it.

Hummingbirds visit flowers to feed on nectar. While they are doing this, their long beaks become covered in pollen, which they then carry to other flowers.

Do it yourself

Find out which colours insects prefer.

1. You need four cards, each a different colour. On the centre of each, place an upturned lid.

2. Pour sugar solution (sugar dissolved in a little water) into the lids. The insects will soon come.

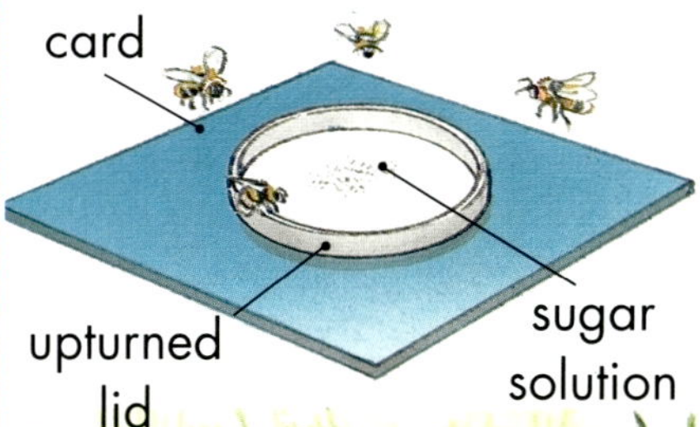

Wind-Blown Pollen

Some flowers rely on the wind to carry pollen. These catkins are groups of male flowers. Each catkin releases up to five million pollen grains to make sure that some of the pollen is carried by the wind to the female flowers.

Eye-Spy

How many different types of flower can you find? Count the petals.

See if the petals are joined together to form a tube, like the lupin, or arranged in a circle, like the campion.

wild rose

honeysuckle

dandelion

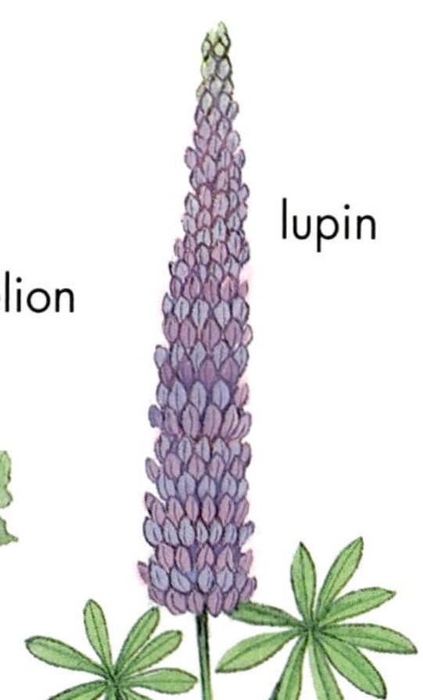
lupin

campion

Fruits and Seeds

Once a flower has been pollinated, it can make seeds. First, the petals and stamens wither and drop off. Then the ovary swells in size and starts to change into a fruit. The seeds develop inside the fruit. A seed is a dry structure, with a hard outer covering called the testa. Inside there is a food store and an embryo which will grow into a new plant.

Cones

Conifers produce cones instead of flowers. The cones contain seeds. As the cone dries out, the scales open and the seeds are blown away.

Eye-Spy

A fruit contains seeds while a vegetable comes from the leaves, roots or stem. How many of each can you think of?

In autumn some plants produce colourful berries that are eaten by birds. Others produce light fruit with fluffy hairs that can float away on the wind.

blackberry

clematis

hawthorn

The Biggest Seed

The fruit of the coco de mer weighs up to 18 kg and contains just one seed. The seed can take nearly 10 years to develop.

Do it yourself

Cones make attractive Christmas decorations.

1. Collect some cones. Make sure they are dry.

2. Dab a little glue on each cone. Sprinkle it with silver or gold glitter, or spray it with silver or gold paint.

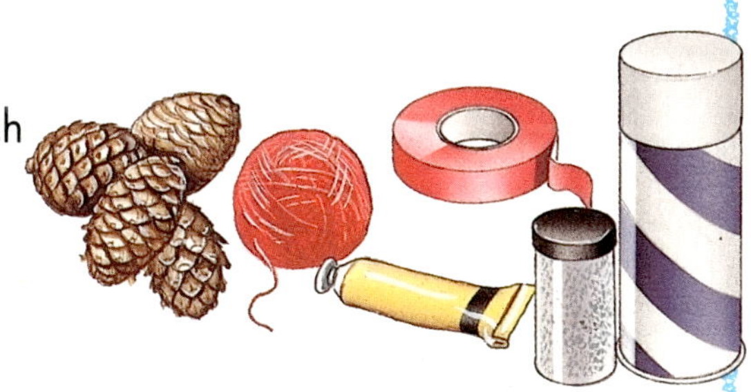

3. Tie some string round the cone and hang it fom the Christmas tree. To make a larger decoration, hang three or four cones together.

4. You can also make table decorations using cones, holly, and red ribbon.

Plants have many clever ways of making sure that their seeds are distributed far and wide. Some plants produce fruits with hairy parachutes, which carry the seeds on the wind. Others have pods that act like slings, catapulting seeds away from the parent plant. Spiky fruits get tangled in animal fur. Brightly-coloured fruits are very tasty, so they are eaten by mammals and birds.

Coconut trees are a common sight on tropical beaches. Their fruits drop into the water and are carried by ocean currents to other shores. There they germinate and grow into trees.

Broom and vetch pods dry and split open, popping out the seeds. The burdock relies on animals to pick up its prickly burrs. The seeds of the dandelion, clematis and sycamore are blown by the wind.

Edible fruits

Brightly-coloured fruits are sweet-tasting, so that they will be eaten by animals. The seeds are passed out in the animal's droppings and dispersed over a large area.

sycamore

Eye-Spy

How many different ways of dispersing seeds can you find amongst the flowers growing in your garden or local park?

Do it yourself

Pumpkins are very large fruits that you can grow yourself. At Hallowe'en, it is fun to hollow one out and put a candle inside.

1. Choose a sunny part of the garden. Mix plenty of compost into the soil to provide nutrients for the plant. Sow the seed in late spring. As the plant grows, make sure it has plenty of water.

2. The plant will produce separate male and female flowers.

3. To get fruits, you may have to to pollinate the female flower, which is the one with swellings behind the petals. Use a small paint brush to pick up pollen from the stamens of the male flower, and rub it onto the stigma in the middle of the female flower. Leave only one fruit on the plant, so that you get a big pumpkin.

The largest-ever pumpkin weighed 400.9 kg. Can you beat this record?

Starting Life

A plant begins its life when the seed germinates. First, the seed absorbs water and swells, causing the seed coat to split open. Inside, the embryo has begun to grow. The root is the first to appear, quickly followed by the shoot. Seeds need the right conditions to germinate. Some tree seeds germinate only after many weeks of cold weather. Some seeds survive for many years in the ground, waiting for the right temperature or for rain.

Eye-Spy

Find a tree standing on its own in a park and look around the base for seedlings. Are there more on one side than the other?

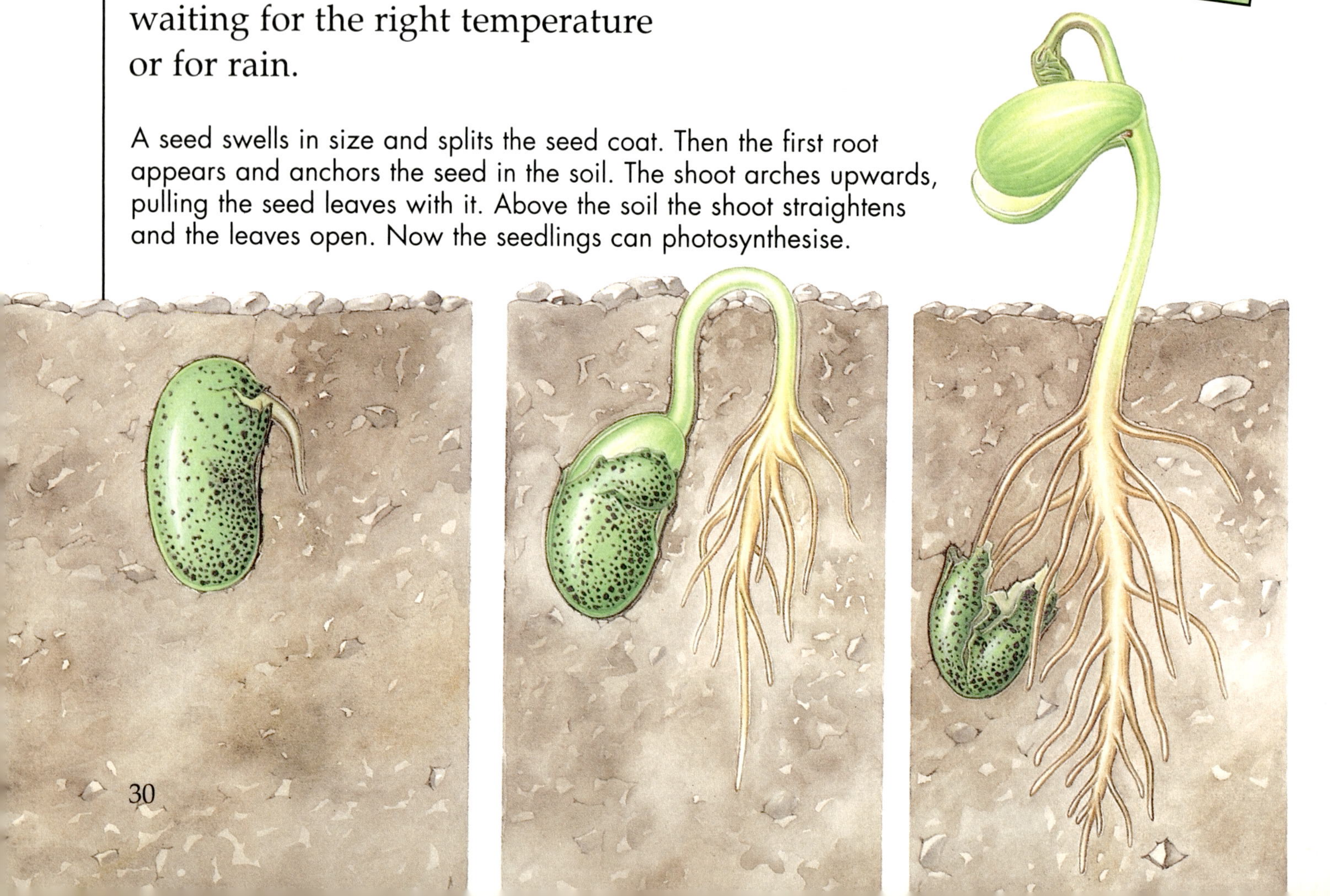

A seed swells in size and splits the seed coat. Then the first root appears and anchors the seed in the soil. The shoot arches upwards, pulling the seed leaves with it. Above the soil the shoot straightens and the leaves open. Now the seedlings can photosynthesise.

Do it yourself

Find the best way to germinate cress seeds.

1. Make a few drainage holes in two plastic tubs. Put kitchen paper in the bottom and soak it with water. Sprinkle in some seeds.

2. Put one tub in the fridge and the other on a sunny window ledge.

3. Leave them for a few days, but make sure that they do not dry out. Add more water if necessary.

How It Works

You should find that the seeds on the window ledge germinate but those in the fridge do not. This is because cress seeds need warm conditions to germinate.

After the Fire

The seeds of the Banksia plant from Australia only germinate after they have experienced high temperatures and smoke from a fire. After the fire there are plenty of nutrients in the ground from the ash, and no other plants to compete.

Index